Survivable World

Survivable World

Ron Mohring

Winner of the
2003 Washington Prize

The Word Works
WASHINGTON, D.C.

First Edition
First Printing
Survivable World
Copyright © 2003 by Ron Mohring

The WORD WORKS
PO Box 42164
Washington, DC 20015
editor@wordworksdc.com

Cover photograph and frontispiece by Fred Wilkinson
"Skypath II" © Fred Wilkinson (www.skypaths.co.uk)
"Skypath IV" © Fred Wilkinson (www.skypaths.co.uk)

Book design, typography by Janice Olson

Library of Congress Number: 2003112324
International Standard Book Number: 0-915380-55-2

Acknowledgments

Thanks to the editors of the following journals in which versions of these poems appear:

Alaska Quarterly Review: "The 'V' in Love"
Art & Understanding: "Afterlife" & "Song for David"
Artful Dodge: "His Hair," "Telling the Family" & "The Woman Who Cleans the Men's Room"
Bay Windows: "This Man"
Blue Moon Review: "The Centaur Eating Windshield Glass" & "Support"
Diagram: "The Mall of the Inevitable" & "San Francisco Zoo"
The Flying Island: "Dead Letter #7"
Gettysburg Review: "This World and All It Holds" & "The Useful Machine"
The Eleventh Muse: "Imagining Us There"
Evergreen Chronicles: "That Day"
Hanging Loose: "Amateur Grief," "Enduring Love" & "PGH Airport"
Modern Words: "Opening"
Phoebe: "Death"
Pivot: "Ever After"
Poems & Plays: "To Have and to Hold"
Puerto del Sol: "Under"

"The Useful Machine" is reprinted in *Things Shaped in Passing: More 'Poets for Life' Writing from the AIDS Pandemic* (Persea Books, 1997)

"San Francisco Zoo" & "The Mall of the Inevitable" are reprinted in *Some from Diagram: Selections from the Magazine & More* (Del Sol Press, 2003)

"PGH Airport" & "Windows" are reprinted in *How to Be This Man* (Swan Scythe Press, 2003)

Several of these poems appeared in the chapbooks *Amateur Grief* (Thorngate Road, 1998, selected by Maureen Seaton for the Frank O'Hara Award), *The David Museum* (New Michigan Press, 2002), and *Beneficence* (Pecan Grove Press, 2003)

for David, and for Randy

CONTENTS

I

II

III

IV

I

Bela Lugosi

Would sift through my window screen,
frizzing violet smoke

that poured into the shape of a man.
Like candle wax on water,

alive as he could be.
I was not like other boys. He knew.

My magic was to leave
no portion of my body bare,

tuck the sheet tight around
my neck. He wouldn't

just bite through; it was the flesh exposed
that provoked his thirst. I'd feel him

at my bedside, open my eyes and stare back
into his, glassy black. Burning to belong,

fearing he'd discard me after.

Opening

It was like floating. Like being outside my body, though not
at first. At first it was like suffocating. Like being small,

having someone big come sit on you, force
a pillow over your face to scare you. It might have been scary

but I was calm. Maybe it was more like drowning,
or slow freezing, how the body gives in. It was

like that: the giving in. It was something I'd accepted.
I could make him stop; that was understood. I knew

I wouldn't. He'd take it as far as he wanted. It was
the being taken. For a while I thought

I was being devoured, swallowed by something
larger, something that held me and would not let me

fall. Like melting, but from the inside out.
Starting with a vagueness, a warmth, not quite burning,

not a place I'd known before. Imagine a hand
passing through your body. Moving. It was like that,

like being opened. Lifted. Cradled. I was the shell
and the heart of the shell, what it curls to protect.

Opening. Unfolding in his hand.

Artery

Each acetate page in the manual
adds layers to the Visible Man: bright organs,
systems, intricate feathery networks:
skeletal, respiratory, circulatory.
Blue for veins. Red for arteries.

I peel gauze dressing from Isaac's hip,
undrape the gaping window.
Position the catch tray. Dribble
peroxide from the bulb syringe
to clean the wound. A patient must

be turned, repositioned every
three hours. The time it takes for skin
to begin its breakdown. The red
bedsores caving in. The opening
that will not close, though we debride

twice daily. Isaac shifts in bed,
lifts the wasted leg. I watch
the ivory ball pivot in its
socket. The rubbery
artery draped over it, pulsing.

The Die-In

He curls on the sidewalk, holds himself
still. I bend to trace his body's outline
with chalk. Always in the same position.

The curling. The kneeling over him.
Recording the crook of his elbow.
The clenched hands. The neck. He opens

his eyes, looks at me. He does not
look away. The chalk marks a rough oval
around his head. I pull him up. The outline

becomes fixed, anonymous. The cops shift
on their horses. He lowers himself again
as though fallen, as though struck down.

I kneel to trace this record, this continual
almost-touching of his body. We will
do this repeatedly until we are stopped.

The Centaur Eating Windshield Glass

Munches reflectively in blue coplight stammer,
tongue dripping. Like swallowing
your own teeth, a mouthful. His whitened eyes
separate: independent beams
grazing first the birthday cake
mashed in its flattened box, then, thrown
across the floorboards, you. You blink.
The centaur is a cop
with the body of a deer:
spindled legs that crumpled instantly
and heaved the rolling weight into the windshield's
collapsing hammock. Another cop asks
Can you move? The first sweeps fractured glass
into his glove, appears to offer
a handful to the stag's blackened muzzle.

AIDS Foundation Resale Center, Houston

Sam, it isn't five yet is it? Have you closed already? God,
it's really hot out there. I'll only stay a minute, listen now:
I was at the church today, no not mine, the Baptist.
Something Temple just off San Jacinto, what's that street?
Well anyway, they're putting in a road. Now Sam
you know how roads are, and right now the place is full
of standing water. Look at my rubbers, they're covered

with mud. You can't leave water standing, it breeds mosquitoes.
While I'm here, I need a wide tie, he said he likes wide ties,
the new minister, what have you got? What?
Well, I went next door and asked the man for a hoe
to cut a ditch. Sam, they'd torn up all these flowers,
I don't know the name, I thought moss roses but these
have fleshier leaves, succulent, and little orange petals, quarter-inch

wide, the man said purslane but I think he doesn't know.
Here, I've got one in my sweater. Can you use these anywhere?
I took bunches home. I think they root real easy. Are you sure?
Okay. Sam, what's the price on this saucepan, I can't read it.
I'm running out of pans to raise my tadpoles in, hundreds right now,
that's really why I came to talk to you, soon as these people go away.
Hey! Your zinnias look awful. If you don't water them

they won't survive the weekend. It would depress your regulars
to see dead flowers; they've got enough on their minds.
Have you got a bucket? I should bring you a yucky bucket.
No one would steal it. This bowl will do. Which way
is the bathroom? I forget. It'll just take a minute . . .
They're really dry, Sam, you know why? It's this overhang.
They don't catch the rain—No, he's closed, come back Monday,

I'm just tending the plants. Let me flip this sign. There, it's past five
and Sam this is what I need: they can't stay outside,
last time my landlord poured them off the porch and they died.
There's nobody else to ask, no one I trust, and Sam you've been
so good to me, please consider it. It's just three days
I'll be away. I could bring them to the store. You won't kill them,
it's easy, just change the lettuce on the second day.

You might have to strain them. Their urea stays in the water.
It's poison. I use a coffee strainer. Pick up the pan,
just turn the whole thing through the strainer, then you put
fresh water in the pan and dump them back. Have you got a sack
for my cart? This one's got some mud—yes, that's fine.
Did I ask you if you liked my hat? This crippled lady at my church
makes them. Well. Her son punches out the beer cans,

but she crochets the whole thing by herself. It folds right up, see?
Tell me that you'll do it, Sam, and I'll do something nice for you.
Maybe I've got something rare you could use here in the store.
You really should read up on it. You won't believe how many times
its weight just one can eat. Filthy parasites don't stand a chance.
Mosquitoes started this whole mess, you know. Green monkeys
my eye! *You* ever been to Africa? Have you found that wide tie?

Death

Arrives at the party late,
of course. His potential partners scatter
    like bowling pins. He wants
to ditch the sickle and hood. He hates
wearing black, is certain yellow would flatter
    his tone. If he could dance

    just once, he'd be the life
of the party. Death hulks behind
    a potted palm, jiggles
the ice in his drink, bored past belief.
They always act surprised to find
    him here. How dull. He wiggles

    a creaky shoulder, taps
his toes. They rattle loose in his shoe
    like dice in a cup. Some nights
it's easy: a guest will just collapse
with fear. Sometimes he has to do
    the work. Of course he's right

    every time; who could deny
that when you're dead, you're dead? Death peeks
    at his watch: it must have quit.
The band is quiet. Useless to try
the old routine of hide-and-seek;
    they saw his crummy outfit

and know it's no disguise.
He sighs: *It's not the good old days.*
    The other plague was fun.
Folks danced and fucked and dropped like flies
but kept the party rolling. Whoever says—
    I mean <u>anyone</u>—

    that life's better today—
well that's a sorry crock of lies.
    I've been there and I <u>know</u>.
These stiffs can't even dance their way—
he points—Get up, you wimp. Surprise!
    It's time. Come on. Let's go.

This World and All It Holds

He sees the way all things contain
themselves, and are contained.
How one cannot escape the other.
The universe, the stars.
The goldfish in its wet globe, fanning.

The snail hauls its shell
up the glass on one foot.
To rest, it must let go.
Evenings, he's watched the snail
unbury itself: the gravel shifting,
small pebbles wedged aside
as the stretching head emerges.

He thinks of his heart
thanklessly working, always emptying
itself, and more blood washing in,
refilling its four small rooms.
The lungs expand. Capillaries
exchange elements. The brain,
the mind divide their tasks.
Resonant gesture. Voracious senses.
Music. Light. The names assigned to all things.

On his porch the spider plant, *mala madre,*
flings away her young. Perpetuation.
The castor bean, lanky jointed umbrella,
distills poison in its speckled seeds.
The figs tear off their crumpled hands
and throw them down. Redbuds pluck
their yellow hearts.

Everything he knows will fall away.
It will feel like sleep.
What remains is inarticulate.

The Woman Who Cleans the Men's Room

Calls hello and pushes through the door.
      Bends to prop it open. Pulls
gloves on, starts at sinks. She hears their shoes
      scrape against the tiled floor,

yanking zippers, quick successive roars:
      flushes meant to override
sounds of passion thwarted. Men who hide.
      Forced to leave, they drop their eyes,

beat a quick retreat. At first she tried
      smiling. Now she doesn't care
what they think. She's seen them here before.
      They're like little boys who've lied:

faces tell so much of who we are.
      Men who never wash their hands,
men in suits. She doesn't understand
      how a person could desire

love like this. The sinks are done. Pretend
      nothing's dangerous. The stalls
next. Not love, but sex. They walk the halls,
      wait for her to finish. Friends

can't believe she keeps the job. The walls
      filthy: stains she's half-afraid
of (despite the gloves), and words she's glad
      not to read. Her husband tells

jokes: *los maricones,* queers. She's heard
          everything, knows what the hole
drilled between these two adjacent stalls
          means. She knows that scouring words

off the tiles won't stop a thing. It's all
          muddled. Like the way she hates
having sex. The smell. Her husband waits.
          When he enters her she feels

dead. Imagines coupled men, holes cut
          through the walls. She's ill. The floor
sinks beneath her. What are women for?
          Better not to ask. She'll scrub all night.

Mercy Fuck

He lived in a trailer with a six-inch-high picket fence
penning a row of ceramic ducks on the lawn and plastic
daisy pinwheels squeaking as they spun in the constant wind.
A tiny red light blinked slowly from a distant hill.
I could barely see its outline in the night. I had no earthly idea
where I was. He was a repeat caller and I had broken
nearly every rule: told him my real name, given him my number,
talked him through weepy late-night calls to my apartment,
and now I squinted beside his ratty gold Buick, watching him climb
the molded fiberglass steps to unlock the trailer door. The inside
made me lurch: so much surface, so many objects
crammed together, velvet pillows heaped on one sofa,
another piled with slithering yellow stacks of National Geographic,
stoppered bottles of colored water everywhere. No place to sit.
I asked to use the john. The door wedged open by a plaster
collie bank sporting a red gingham bow. A hole punched
through its head. *I could die here
and no one would find me.* "Something to drink?" Tom startled me
as I peed while holding up the plush-covered seat. His voice
soft and high, his peach-fuzz mustache,
like a teen's, though he was 43 and had never
been laid. Enter me. *Stupid,*
I told myself after giving directions to my apartment. *Stupid,
stupid,* in his car heading north out of the city. Now Tom
lead me down a cramped hall which seemed
to tilt like in an old Batman episode: the criminal's
lair, the Riddler, the Joker, Egghead. Tom sat, patted the bed.
I stripped quickly and lay on my back. He turned out the light
to remove his clothes, rolled carefully against me, his soft
pudgy ass grazing my arm. "Ah, disappointment," he sighed
in a moment, in a voice that has stayed with me all my life,
haunting me on buses, in restaurants, waiting in line

at the movies. I see a homely man and glance down,
then back, and wonder what it's like to be in a body
you hate, to have a face so ugly
people turn away. And what did I think I could do for this man
who'd never felt another man inside him, who cried on the phone
that next week was his birthday, and the words had come,
astonishing us both. I confess it now:
I thought I was doing him a favor. It doesn't matter
that he wanted it too. I don't know what it meant to Tom,
but for the next ten years I said yes to any man who asked,
as if I could reverse disgust, as if from generosity
and not a kind of shame. Is Tom alive today?
I remember how he breathed in grunting gasps,
how I thought about the long drive back
and tried not to rush anything. I wanted him to feel it.
I think there's a cruelty in presumption. I think it's in us all.
Sometimes I wish there'd been a man
who fucked me purely out of pity.
So I'd never forget how that feels.

Ever After

Because they know the way it ends,
his sister's children ask to hear
the story read to them again,

but starting in the middle, when
the danger peaks. And though it's clear
(because they know the way it ends)

the hero will prevail again,
they love to squeal and huddle near.
The story, read to them again,

provides some danger but amends
the rules: they're all protected here.
Because they know. The way it ends

is this: the uncle and his friend
will both be gone within a year.
The story, read to them again

by someone else, won't seem the same.
They'll close the book. Won't want to hear,
because they know the way it ends,
the story read to them again.

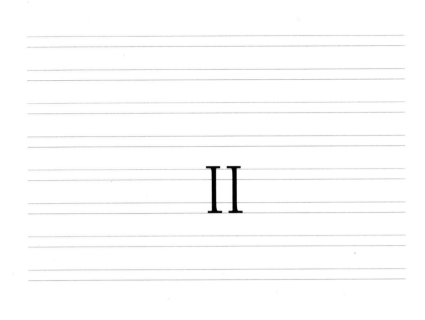

II

The 'V' in Love

The **v** in love divides the word:
It's **lov,** we say. We sing it out,
a single note we want to hold,
unfold, extend in range. We forget

the coiled **e,** eating quietly
its tail, hungry ghost that eyes
not the slender **l,** the keen sharp **v,**
but instead the appetizing

o, so fat, so filling, so
necessary to the whole
experience—and isn't **o**
the undisputed heart of all

we mean? Don't we love to murmur
O, and **o,** our mouths round
with pleasure? How love sounds.
How silent the **e** at the end, its closure.

Song for David

Waking, he shudders, wrenches free
as one yanks a shoe from sucking mud
wet with fear, the sheets
dark with night sweat,
and lunges from the dream to cling to me.

To comfort but not reassure, to be
as close as I can bear, stay open,
yet withhold some space
that's mine alone, to let
the nightmare edges tear reality,

to comprehend that I will let him go—
though not tonight,
not yet—I know my place:
it's here with him. (And then. . . ?) I understand

what haunting will become, but cannot know
if what will linger here
will be a trace
of him, or me. I fumble for his hand.

The Process

Walking after David's call.
Moon a gold sliver, parachute
in a tree. Early frost
has killed the wandering jew
neglected on the porch.

In my neighbor's house
a party's winding down. People spill
in pairs onto the lawn. I watch until
the lights wink out.

David's in Ohio, a funeral, our ninth
friend dead this year. This has to stop,
I say, though of course it doesn't;
sometimes I fear we'll all go down.
It's hard to think ahead.

Last week we argued in group.
David had swayed them: we both
should go, importance of grief, give in
to the process. I was obdurate. Polly,
our therapist, said gently: *Hon, we ain't
got time to fuck around.* I walked out.

Cold. The last roses disintegrate
in the garden. I touch an open blossom;
it shatters. I remember the bouquet
I took to Stephen, his fingers
stroking petals as I described
each color he couldn't see.

Imagining Us There

Two moons in the violet sky. Three moons.
Air thick as honey we move
through, no longer needing to inhale,
exhale, all we require
absorbed through our new mottled skins.
Your head held
between my hands as if it were a shell, as if
what it contained

were irreplaceable. No need in this place
for speech.
Our mouths unnecessary but for this
ritual we share:
our tongues reach for each other
as if they longed
to leave our ruined bodies, as if they were
creatures we merely

harbored, that we had the power to release.
The lesions vanish.
Your body takes on weight. Facial bones retreat
beneath the skin;
peripheral vision returns. The hard beads
of your spine
are blanketed once more. Once more we slide
together without fear,

our bodies lubricous, pale blue beneath
the moons that circle
this planet, spill their gauzy light upon us.
Your head moves
as if I were guiding you. I am opening
from the inside out.
I am closing my eyes. We are dreaming this place.
You are taking me.

Into Mine

I watch the fish glide in their tank. It lowers
the blood pressure, you tell me, but sometimes
I think I might throw a paperweight against
the glass, though I know I'd be sorry; it would
pain me to see them bleed, gaping on the
sodden carpet. Not for that. For the moment
before that, the huge collapse and rush
as they're poured from their survivable world.

Losses

The mouse discovered in the sweater drawer
does not wrestle with decisions. Before
I've reached the attic and brought down

a box suitable for transfer, she's gone.
The rubbery pink babies wriggle, blind.
What now? I'm frozen by her stark response,

resist its blunt efficiency. I don't need
the sweater, don't even like it. I'll go without.
I want her to come back, carry them off

as a mama cat nips her young by their necks,
trots away dangling their limp bodies. Her
lesson's clear: Cut your losses, begin again.

Dying Time, Living Time

1.   The Edge of This

As if one could discern the moment.

How you watch him sleep: the hands'
premonitive fold upon the chest,

the afternoon light fading. His closed
eyes flickering. *Watch out,* your parents

would call as you pumped higher on the swing,
and you'd slow down, believing you'd sidestep

disaster by seeing it coming. How life now
slows, the planet itself braking

until you feel your heels grind dirt, time
taking its time, an unspeakable lurch

curdling in your throat: *make it quick,*
make it soon. Welded to your chair, you watch:

Is this his last good day?
Vigilance has no idea how utterly

this death will scrape you raw,
scathe you with its rigor.

2.   *Window Table*

David's sunglasses, frames crossed, blue cord
looping off the table. His book closed,
a torn envelope's edge marking a page
near the middle. His chair pushed back.
His glass of melting ice pools a ring of water.
Empty plate. A line of customers snakes
from counter to door, their voices climbing
over one another, above the kitchen's clank
and hiss. I am reading the upside-down
jacket blurb but it makes no sense. Almost
winter. We are heading to the hospital
but have stopped for lunch. David always
does this, insisting that we eat despite the news,
despite the urge to scream. We must wash,
we must eat, we must drive the car. Avoid
pedestrians. A man in a black T-shirt
holds his daughter, rocking. Across the street
workers rake gravel beside an absurdly small
bulldozer, bright yellow. A man takes
our plates, our water. Wipes the table.
I didn't look up. I never saw him walk away.

PGH Airport

It is not the red-faced man
wearing dirty Reeboks and matching Illinois State

T-shirt and shorts. It is not
the man in the lime polo shirt who grabs at his clip-on

pager. It is not the tall man
in the white shirt carrying a Faulkner novel who eyes me frankly

but does not stop to say hello.
Not the small Brazilian man with the black elastic band

wrapped around his head,
the bright wire mouth guard gleaming. Not the loping man

in soft gray cowboy boots
and drooping black felt hat, though he's passed this spot four times.

Not the man in the leather shop
with heavy silver loops in his ear. Behind a row of video screens

announcing departures,
a pair of muscled legs. It is not the man attached.

It is neither of the mustached ones
in matching Pittsburgh T-shirts, nor the businessman

carrying his metal briefcase.
Not the bearded man with his cap turned backward who smiles

as I stare, though for a moment
I think it could be him. The flight attendant with perfect hair,

the Greek man in the cobalt shirt
listening to his headphones, the Asian man in the yellow mesh

tank top, arms and chest fluid, solid:
none will deliver me. The Greek man bites his nails.

White bunched socks.
Mole above his lip. He is so beautiful, I can't understand

why no one has found him.

Amateur Grief

Driving home on 288, where I like to scream because in this traffic
who's to know? There's just time enough to fix dinner
for his family or take them to Taco Cabana or Wok & Roll,
everyone strained, polite—after ten years you'd think we'd know
whether we liked one another—but of course that doesn't
matter now. Time to eat, shower off
the fear and drive back to the hospital, traffic streaming
over the little rise, downtown and the Galleria glittering at dusk,
Houston so flat that any excuse for a hill affords a view. The kids
in Hermann Park climb the artificial slope at the outdoor theater

just to scream and hurl themselves back down and I swear
it's the only place in this city you can do that; we'd watch them
and thank god we were childless queers. Evening dropping
fast, truck windows open for noise, for the rush of fumed air
that passes for a breeze. It's January and seventy,
forty by the weekend they say. I'm thinking about the gaggle
of strangers and how they were all related:
the doctor stepped from the ICU, called the family name and eleven
people bent to his attention, and a boy sitting with a woman
pointed to me on the floor, my back against a potted ficus,
and asked *Why doesn't he get up?*
and the woman said *He's here for someone else.*

Radio off then on, more sound to scream into, should anyone notice
they'd mutter something about road rage and maybe steer
a little clear, and the sky this morning a startling blue as we left
our cars for the building, pigeon shit ruining the sidewalk,
and his mother said *Viruses and pigeons*
will come to rule the earth and I thought *They're already here.*
I looked up and thought, *This would be a good day to go.* We're flying
fast enough to kill ourselves, obliterate each other with one swerve,
how many in this rushing mess are gripping tight, thinking the same?

Only yesterday I was weeping in Kroger, in the produce aisle,
in the filthy bathroom, dead center in this neighborhood of queers
and where else is it safe to have your little breakdown, hon?
Right here is fine, right now, wind whipping road-grit in my face,
skyscrapers flushing all coppery and pink, big curved mirrors
we can see through, all those office lights, so many working, do they
watch the sun plummet, splash us with this light? It's almost bursting,
this space we're moving in is brimming, it can't be contained, and I'm
caught by the light, caught *in* it, I can't help myself, I'm still
so much in love with the physical world.

Intubation

The doctor sweeps in, parts the flutter
of nurses, barks for a portable x-ray, *Stat!*

> *Thread him through this passage.*

squarely parks his face before David's
to hastily propose our only option:

> *O Stern Captain,*

pass a tube into the bronchial
pipe, attached to a machine—a "ventilator"—

> *stranger in whom we place*

a hope, a breath,
unburden the drowning lungs. Reversible,

> *all hope and trust,*

he says, also *Emergency*. Chest heaving,
mask clamped to his face,

> *by these instruments*

David—all eyes—manages assent:
Whatever—you have—to do—not knowing

> *deliver him to me.*

the procedure will prevent speech. We
have ten more minutes, and everything to say.

That Day

The rooms are arranged like spokes in a wheel,
I think, and his is not the center.
The nurses' station is the center. The charts, the monitors.
The nurses, the doctors move in and out of this center,
the command center, and the rooms orbit this center.
Like wagons in a circle. Protect us.
Like petals of a daisy. He hears me he hears me not.
Like a satellite, a space station. What place is this?
How came we here? What planet so cruelly identical,
save one man's life, to the home we were yanked from?
The rooms arranged in a ring,
each holding a body. The man in the next room improving,
but I can't feel joy for his family. Because it isn't David.
How the name *David* balances on the pivot of its *V*,
a *D* at each end, the vowels facing, *A, I.*
David. Gravid, livid. Fervid. Avid.

The specialized mattress circulates ice water
to lower his fever. Fever. Lower. Layer. Lover.

Dead skin crusts his lips, a mouth-mask I could peel,
press to my face like a scar.

Six plastic bags dangle, trapeze suicides
giving up their fluids—take us; spare him—
but his body's a mess, tubes shoved up
his penis, down his throat, as if in punishment for how he got
this way. . . *Oh Lil,*
my mother's elderly friend Bonnie
would moan those days she felt a wreck,
I feel like a busted asshole. His hands balloon,
horrifically swollen. His searing fever soars. His frothy lungs

have given up, must be forced by this wheezing machine.
So invasive, these extraordinary measures we've pinned
against his going. Could I worm
behind those twitching
eyelids, find instruction there? Are you
winging it, love? Have you an escape
planned? Can you stand the unvoiced pain?
As if on command, the night nurse pushes for relief:
he floats, unhoused, in morphine's numbing arms.

III

His

hair in the brush. His mail
by the door: his tongue
on the envelope, spit in the glue.
His truck in the driveway, keys

on the hook. His clothes
in the closet. His pills
on the night stand. His name
on the lease, books on the desk.

His cat wanting in. Wanting out.
His film in the camera.
His address book. Figs from his tree
in the freezer. His plants needing

water, his shoes in the hall.
His furniture. His watch, his ring.
His tanks of fish. His silence.
His family to call.

Telling the Family

It was not the virus, but the opportunistic infections.
He never wanted you to worry. He swam too far
and couldn't fight the undertow. It pained him

that you never called. He slammed his car into a bridge.
He insisted on flying alone—a sudden downdraft
swatted him into Lake Michigan. He was afraid

he might go blind. The virus had entered his brain.
The water heater exploded. He fell from the extension ladder
while cleaning the gutters. His neck. He walked out

into the deepening snow and just kept going. The twister
lifted off the roof and plucked him from his chair.
It was nothing specific. He left a note and swallowed

all his medications. He'd talked it over
with his doctor. His face covered with lesions.
The intruder slashed his throat. He died of boredom.

The bridge collapsed. It was something in the water.
It was a sudden stroke. Food poisoning. He'd lost
his job. It was the shock of seeing

through you. He'd had the same pneumonia
twice before. It's been in all the papers;
you must have heard of it by now. Lightning,

it was lightning. His liver failed. No one knew
he'd bought the gun. He had time to arrange everything.
He never knew. It was a blessing. He dropped

seventy pounds. Choked on a piece of plastic.
Yanked out all the tubes. Fell on his sword.
He would have wanted you to know.

Lingering

Flattened, purple, the size of a button, more wart
than bruise, it doesn't hurt. I check daily,
prod it with my finger, dare it to change
or go away. It remains implacable as a toad.
There are no others. It could be something else. I can't tell.

:   :   :   :   :

Sunday Eurydice soiled the bed. I woke
to the warm stench of shit. She lay curled
over my arm. I wiped her clean, stripped
the quilts. Last week the vet said three months.
She doesn't seem to be in any pain. By the time
David's cat died, he'd moved her into a room
lined with newspapers. There are things
you simply do, he said, but I can't make
this choice. Nights, I listen to the house
and can't distinguish what's inside my mind,
what's in the wind. David asked to be placed
in the garden. I think of the young pear trees,
their roots fingering fragments of bone. I can't.

:   :   :   :   :

Does having a place to go assist our return?

:   :   :   :   :

As a child I rode in the back of the station
wagon, fell asleep hearing the tires, the road
repeating sounds. Voices. An urgent, ongoing

discussion. I believed they were my
ancestors. I knew they talked about me.
I slept, completely in their hands.

    :   :   :   :   :

Imagine: the molecules of our bodies dance like the edges of clouds,
wavering, always that close to leaving us, always falling away.
Surely something of ourselves remains with the objects we touch;
something must linger. Sometimes when I lie still I feel the bed
quiver the exact beat of my heart. As if my body did not end.
As if I were contained in a husk that might dissolve at any
moment. I close my eyes. I listen.

What I Fear

You tap the window. I'm buried
in my thoughts. The screen door bangs.

I walk out to the garden bench,
look for the moon. You're touching me,

saying my name. I hear the ritcheting
small frogs, the ones I saved as tadpoles

from the flooded street this spring.
Their tiny see-through bellies looked,

you'd said, like thumbprint whorls.
I'd imagined clocksprings. It's months now

since the last frog was released, though
I tried to keep one back for you to see.

After leaving your room, walking out
in the rain, I turned in the parking lot

and found your window. They had flipped you
like a board against the rails. Two of them

were cutting off your clothes. They were
rolling you back. Someone was closing

your mouth. I opened mine,
felt rain on my face.

San Francisco Zoo

I am watching David through a dirty window.
It's pouring rain, and children dash through the runoff,
a dripping curtain. Inside the carousel house

they scramble astride the animals. David circles,
aiming his camera. One girl can't decide. The carousel

begins to move and her mother plops her quickly
on an ostrich. David steps back as the enormous wheel spins
into a blur of surfaces, strings of lights, revolving

mirrors. One boy's pleading for a photo, posing differently
each turn: kneeling in the saddle, holding on with one arm,

head flung back, riding low off one side of his pony.
The boy tries to stand in the saddle but the attendant,
in khakis and safari helmet, rushes up and makes him sit.

Cheap speakers pop and shudder, blast out organ music.
We have changed buses four times. We have hurried

past the bears pacing outside their caves, their great
wet bodies rippling. The pure swans seem oblivious,
rain, no rain, it's all the same, blinking their clear eyelids,

dipping bright beaks in the water. The carousel slows.
David changes film, kneels beside a pair of spotted cats,

each with a fish in its mouth. This is our last vacation,
David's last birthday. We have no idea. I will
find the film saved in a plastic bag.

The Useful Machine

*"Look at the
useful machine I built instead of grieving."*
Rachel Wetzsteon

Programmed to operate without commands, this amazing unit
practically thinks for itself. Sensitive as the delicate, twitchy hands

of a Geiger counter, but more discreet—no blinks, no whistles
nor bells—it efficiently searches and finds the particular stimuli

invisibly linked to my suggestible moods. It reads my mind
like a map. Better than. In short, it *knows*. The sun this afternoon

blares through the blinds, backlights the Easter cactus that grows,
despite neglect, on the table. The light reveals the plant's insides:

a central spine, the thinnest ribs. Before I know
what I feel, before I'm able to think the word *x-ray,*

a Sousa march intended to conceal the image I recall
snaps on in my brain. I override, remember anyway:

I'd lie beside *X* in the narrow bed too small for both of us,
and lightly place my head against his chest. A monitor in the wall

would beep at brief intervals as it fed what *X*'s nurse, a Miss
Lamar, had dubbed his "grocery list." I liked the way she smiled,

how once she said *Now that's a cozy picture.* A green tank hissed
its careful load of oxygen. She walked with a prominent

limp. I'd forgotten her voice. Of course, it's this machine:
it won't let me feel sad. Adroit, it intercepts calls,

well-meaning friends who drop by unannounced
to cook and clean, who feel obliged to force me into chatter:

the weather, which teams were trounced in the NFL. They're worse
than television. But I refuse to be bounced on the knees of the kind;

I'll make my own decisions. I'm tired of hearing the same advice
presented by people who don't even grasp my situation:

*Is it feed a cold and starve a fever or starve a cold and feed
a fever?* Feed a man who burns with fever, feed his fever,

feel how hot then cold his body speeds through cycles like a washer,
wringing out the sweat. His bony frame chattered like clothespins

stuck to a twanging line. Forget yourself. Forget your needs,
or think of them constantly, but go without. Careen from hope

to doubt and back again. What can it mean when strangers wish
you luck? They say a silver cord connects the soul, a plucky

astronaut spacewalking—mother-may-I?—a threaded
rehearsal of imminent flight. The precise moment the tether

breaks is when the body's lost. Soul floats free, a snapped kite.
I'm speaking once again of X. I wanted him to die, to be

unchangeable. The machine is a lie. I planned to help if I had to.
What does this make me?

To Have and To Hold

Not you, I know, not any part of you
I ever knew, which makes me feel somehow

inadequate, as if I should have noticed
every bone, the way I memorized

their names in ninth grade biology,
Mrs. Butts incanting *humerus, radius, ulna.*

I should have seen through you
to the parts that would endure,

carpals, tarsals, phalanges of hands and feet
shattered, sifted and accompanied

by this bronze washer embossed
with your initials, *D, E, W,* and the number

5961, meaning I guess you were almost
the six thousandth—client?—customer?—that yours

was close to the six thousandth body
they burned. Someone logged this, someone

packaged the grit and ash and certified it yours,
femur, tibia, fibula. Patella. Fifty-nine, sixty-one:

they sandwich the year I was born, combine
to form a number unforgivable. On the washer's

reverse, *12395*, the date you were reduced to this.
Except it wasn't you. You'd gone before

the funeral, before the doctor signed
you dead, switched off the machine

bullying your lungs. I would touch your skull—
frontal, parietal, occipital—and mourn what it

contained, what couldn't last, knowing
this receptacle was all that would remain,

gutted bowl and useless frame kiln-fired, fractured,
packaged and delivered to my living hands.

Turning Away

At first innocently, the way after sex he always rose at once
to wash, use the bathroom, wash again, allowing me barely time,

I discovered, to bring myself off again just seconds before he came
back to bed. My hand, my belly sticky. Exertion of calming

my breath, covering what I'd done. I told myself that if
he caught me I'd just laugh—*Of course,*

don't you?—but I always had just enough time,
yanking, tensing my legs till the muscles cramped

and burned, sometimes never really getting hard again, half-
closing my eyes. I wanted more. At last I realized

he had to know, was pushing me to do this without him.
This was his gift. I see it now, the way I see him folding into bed,

rolling to one side. I'd shove against him for a moment—he fell
asleep so quickly—before I turned, hugged the space

that lay before me. Our bodies bent away
from one another, our spines like cogs not touching.

Story

Bobby's propped by pillows, reading fairy tales. Television's on
without the sound. It's accidental that I brought him something
he'd enjoy: at first I thought "easy to read" meant pictures,
and sneaked in a sack of porn. "Oh, *please*," he wailed. "In case
you hadn't noticed, they ran a tube up my weenie!" (He hiked
his gown; I tried to look away.) "How can I—how can *you*—
think of sex?" And so I dragged in all the story books I had.

Bobby cackles and coughs, tips up his foggy mask, hawks
into a Kleenex. Castles and frogs bore him; what he likes best
is gore: a horse, decapitated, sings advice; a desperate stepsister
slices off her heel. Bobby hates Pooh. Forgivable, I say,
because Dottie Parker hated him *more*: "Tonstant Weader
frowed up." He howls into a coughing fit. That he should love
old fairy tales does make a perverse sense. They'd unnerved me
as a child: the Little Prince's lonely planet, jealous witches flying
into rages. How could Red Riding Hood slide down the wolf's
gullet, then reappear intact, every lock in place?

Bobby's nickname—CatWoman—was thoroughly earned.
But he introduced me to David. They were breaking up.
The truth is it wouldn't have mattered, the truth is that we—
David and I—dumped Bobby like the trash he's always been.
We toasted his departure with champagne. Moved to Houston.
Ten years later, David died. Last month Bobby phoned. I think
he wants two things—validation and escape—in more or less equal
portions. Yes, I took his lover. They would have left
each other anyway. He can't forgive me. He's afraid of pain.
He's the only one alive who's known David as I have. There should
be more than this between us.

Bobby never mentions David. He'd rather die
than let me own his story. Who wants to see the end?
—Not I. Not Bobby, who can't avoid the narrative sarcoma's
printing on his skin. ("Just connect the spots!" he says.) The past
keeps turning up, refutes explanation—or else embraces them all.
Every story has another perversion. The Frog Prince missed
the well he'd left behind. The boy who went too far for love
was lost and never seen again. Someone has to tell this.

Dead Letter #7

The swallowtail's back, flits
and shimmies above the garden as if trying
to select from the dazzle: molten lantana, brilliant
red pentas, rampant pink coneflowers, yarrow everywhere.

Tiger? Zebra? Which is which, and where's
the field guide you'd keep on the table? This black-striped
butterfly's an aching yellow, looks just like last year's—is that
possible?—and skips over the bristly clump of borage

ransacked by gangs of bees to light
at the muddy dribble where I've watered in
new basils. Why, I'd like to ask, are there
tomato hornworms on the untouched daylilies,

and if not the lilies, what have they eaten to grow
so green and fat? I have no tomatoes to protect,
lack the heart to squash these striped marauders.
There's fennel and dill enough

for all to eat. Perhaps I'll move them there. What moth
is it these monsters become? You'd tell me Sphinx
I think. I think of you in the lawn chair
in the shade, not reading but watching me work:

your steady gaze, your wide-brimmed hat I laughed at
but wear now. You napping in the house,
me in the hot sun, weeding, watering,
kneeling to examine a swallowtail chrysalis, silk-stirruped

upside-down to a stalk of fennel. This is what
you wanted to be part of. The spring you died
I sank into the garden, planted roses too closely—
better to have more of them I thought—

and purchased impulsively a bottlebrush tree just like
the ones we'd seen in San Francisco, their scarlet
spiky plumes like something out of Oz . . .
Even as I hauled it to the truck I heard your catty

Where will you put it? The question I'd have
to answer convincingly before you'd consent to buy
more plants. I found a place
beside the blueberries. Watering in the tree, I watched

a black-and-yellow swallowtail arc over the crape myrtles,
circle the mint bed twice before lighting
at the feeder. I thought it was you
who'd sent it, to remind me of my promise

that if some part of you could come back, this place
is where I'd watch for it. Three years now and I've almost stopped
talking to you here. I'm nearly ready to keep
that other promise, release what's left of you

to the garden: this brimming excess, the bees
so heavy with pollen they must be exhausted. Flung
into wind, dust and grit latching in needles and leaves,
you'd sink with the rain, rise again everywhere.

The Mall of the Inevitable

David gave these gryphon candlesticks to Craig,
who promptly died and left them to his lover, John.
Before he phoned the family, John lifted
the gryphons from Craig's mantel. David helped
select a funeral suit from the closet, while I rummaged
gingerly through the drawers beneath Craig's platform bed.

Keep looking, said John, *you'll know what for when you find it.*
Then, breaking into sobs: *He just wanted a little
more time!* David held out a tuxedo jacket. My hand
closed on something squashy wrapped in cellophane:
I pulled out the most enormous pink dildo
I'd ever seen, thicker than my arm. Held it up, blushing.
That would be it, said John. *Can't have the mother finding that.*
Then softly to David: *He never got to try it out.*

John died at home the following spring,
attended by his ex-wife Anne and former lover, Buzz.
One day Buzz dropped by our house, handing me
two heavy paper sacks—John's gardening books—
and gave David the candlesticks and John's bishop's ring.
Buzz got John's apartment, died there three years later.

How to diagram the vectors of promise and loss
among David and his friends? Patrick was David's executor
but Patrick died first. David gave Patrick's car to Jim, who died next.
Craig and David and John promised to be there for one another.
David loved those gryphon candlesticks. When he finally
gave them to Craig, was it with foreknowledge of reinheritance?
If you love something, give it away: it will come back
to you, but dragging sorrow. In these times, we loved.

I remember most the weekend the Quilt came to town:
colorful circus of loss, memorial grid laid across the Convention
Center floor. Walking those canvas aisles, it was easy to parse
one's intake of grief: simply focus on one block at a time, and—
as in any war—keep your head down. But I made the mistake
of wandering upstairs. Drawn to a porthole window large and deep

enough to cradle a sleeper, I looked at the enormity below—
the staggering rush of more than I could name—
then stumbled back down to find David photographing
the panel he'd made for Patrick. John was there,
bony and gaunt. He said he'd stopped counting. I felt like
some kind of fraud, a glitch spit out by a chewing beast intent
on swallowing them all. Craig shuffled up in his leather jacket,
his eyes a little scary. He grabbed John's hand: *Let's get out of here.*

IV

Afterlife

After the funeral, after the families disperse,
after the first night alone, and the next,
the first year; after the first man you allow
to touch you, after the tenth, after you let
yourself use the word *love* with someone else,
after you decide to sell the house
but can't get around to it, after you forget
the taste of his ashes and grit on your tongue
and it's easier to say his name, read his diaries,
spend his money, sell his car, fuck
in his bed; after you've rolled the platitudes
into little pills and swallowed them all,
and life presents not cruelty but *experience*,
and his death has become just
another part of you you sometimes ignore,
after that, there is always
your own.

Garden

Almost November, and I'm finding animals in the garden,
the small creatures we barely notice. Flecked snails
hunker into soil, depositing milky eggs. Fat toads

buried under weedy litter, bony snouts like stones
spring to life: golden eyes pop open as they scramble
away from the teeth. Slow anoles huddle in the leaves I rake

from the blackberry bed. I pick one up, hold it in my open hand.
It blinks, shifts, draped across my spread fingers, picking up
my warmth. White belly, ribs heaving like an old man's.

Body changes color, slowly, starting at the feet: pale flush
replaces dead-leaf brown. Eyes close, now blue-ringed.
It lightens. Becomes completely green, the exact shade of the last

new apple leaves. Pivots its head, scrapes its face
along my thumb. Braces and leaps into the blackberry canes.
Then I see the knotted snake squeezed between two beams,

coiled like an ear in a shadow box, listening to the cold. I touch it
with my trowel—it unsprings, twists into the grass, half-gone before
I pin its body, rip grass, diminish its hold and clamp behind

the head, pick it up. The snake flicks out a black-tipped tongue,
wraps my hand, threads my fingers. Such cold muscle. I fear its head
shape, distrust the delicate tongue: measuring, measuring me.

This Man

With his breath
fogs my skin, then watches
his traces erase. I am a window
he sees into, a house in which
the lamps are coming on again.
Shuttered, cinched,
I had made my bed of boards.
In this hardest year
I would be stone. He smiles,
unlocks me
with his tongue.

Enduring Love

A softening grape I toss with a limp
thump, rolling like an eyeball into the sink.
A heaped sheet in the corner that looks
like a body, and I think, *body*,
and only later, *sheet*. A bright pink clump
of canna blossoms bent double,
screaming in the rain. My new boyfriend says I don't
put enough teeth to his foreskin, tells me
he knew a man who wanted his nuts chewed,
mashed until they grew formless and soft.
The secret to enduring love, he says, is shifting
the axis of power. We are on the kitchen table.
I have filled his willing bottom
with cold green grapes and now
he is giving them back to me. The edgy knives
hide in their block. I glance out the window:
the postman in his wet poncho
starts up the walk. Whatever I once thought
of innocence, I know I can no longer plead it.

Lady Death

This time I know who it will be:
sirens spiraling two houses down,
EMTs pumping Mr. Phillips' chest,
Randy naked at the parted curtain,
telling what unfolds. Blinking neighbors
on their lawns, awkward and useless
as furniture; the street crew digging
a hole, methodical, not even
pausing. *Men at Work,* Randy says, meaning
both teams, one urgent and the other
what? Indifferent? Or just playing
their part: some rescue, some watch, some die
and some just dig. Me, I can't decide
where I belong. *Forty years,* I'm thinking,
fifty: that's how long these folks
have stayed put. I've lived here just twelve,
long enough to see them
disappear. The ribs crack
during chest compression, Randy says.
Mr. Kubeczka last fall, before that
Mrs. Doyle. My David that same year,
though not of age. Mr. Curry, then
his wife. Mr. Root. The nameless woman
up the street who lived so long
without running water they simply yanked
the tub and toilets out instead of scrubbing.
How sad, I said, but David
disagreed: *She kept her house*
until she died. I say good for her!
And each time Ruby walked
from house to house, yellow umbrella

bobbing in the rain, in the stunning
heat, collecting signatures and cash
for flowers. We took to calling her
Lady Death, especially the year
cancer bleached and stripped
her body down; the only time she didn't call
was for David, but she was starting chemo.
Five weeks later she found me out
in the garden: rickety, shrunken,
two sweaters flapping, she shuffled past
the wet azaleas to hug me and say
Throw it all away,
his clothes, his shoes. I'm telling you
it's better in the long run. That summer
I thought she might go next, but pressed her
a twenty for Tom's wife and said,
Not you. Ruby blushed. I wonder if she hates
this task? She's the only one who's met
the families who buy these emptied houses,
change the locks, change the neighborhood,
if that's what we have. I don't feel
part of it. Perhaps it's gone, or maybe
it's part of what she does, maintaining
such a ritual, connecting us, strangers
despite ourselves.

Pouring Tea

The way it seems to wrinkle backward
pouring forth, as if undecided,
as if this liquid had a mind,
a soul; could choose: if not to not go,
then to flow more slowly, to savor
its translocation from the greater
to the smaller, more limited container.

Windows

Because I didn't know exactly what I was doing, I succeeded.

Because I have a homo sensibility, and thought: Well that looks nice
but what if I started with much smaller pieces?

Because for months on end I never picked it up, it's still unfinished.

One-inch squares cut from every fabric I could find.
Framed by scalloped muslin folds. The tiny stitches I learned
to make. The muslin blocks vary in shade and texture, at least
four kinds, because I didn't know how much I'd need.

Take a four-inch square of unbleached muslin. Press in half.
Stitch an eighth-inch seam along both narrow ends.

Mother's yellow kitchen curtains. My sister Jenny's handmade dress.
A bag of vintage scraps sent by my now-dead aunt, horrid
clashing patterns, wild smears clipped and squared, made tame
by simple reduction. Everything goes in and all of it belongs.

At first, the challenge of not repeating a single fabric pattern.
Then the math: impossible to count, keep track. Impossible to find
that many samples, though Mother mailed batches, a short note
and tumble of scraps from a squashy envelope.

Pull open the rectangle so it purses along the unstitched sides
and the seams meet at a middle point. Line up the raw edges.
Stitch a seam two-thirds their length from each end,
leaving the middle unsewn.

At a quilt shop, Mother brags about my project. The owner bristles:
But it's not a true quilt. There's no batting, and no quilting to speak of.
It should truly be called a <u>coverlet</u>. Yes, I nod. But want to say
Lady, who gives a shit?

Because it was something to do with my hands
on the airplane, in the waiting rooms, in the vinyl hospital chair.
Watching David sleep. The gooseneck lamp casting enough light
     to work by,
the basket of scraps in my lap. Stitching. Folding. Thinking:
He is dying and this is all I know to do.

Turn the piece inside out and smooth the seams. You should have
a square. Whipstitch the center closed. Now bring one corner point
to the center and tack in place. Repeat for the other three corners.

The flight attendant, the receptionist, a small boy in the hospital
waiting room: *What are you making? May I see?* And I thought:
I am a man who sews in public. Not as performance, and despite
 my fear of ridicule. I find my seat on the bus, in the auditorium,
 and I pull out my sewing.

Sewing. Quilting. Piecework. Salvage.

Because nothing planned is random. I tried to use whatever square
I'd pull next from the basket. Two reds. Green then blue gingham
then three blocks down the same green. But the patterns, the colors
set up their own dialogue. The crimson from one piece
called to the gray pinstripe in the next. Flecks of that same gray
in a blue-green floral. Conjunctions. Associations.
Constellations in an unbleached field.

You will need to make hundreds of these.

At the fabric store, Mother's friends ask: *Is he still working on that*
     quilt?

Because I could not throw them away—David's shirts, the buttons clipped off, saved in a porcelain box, the sleeves removed so I'd never try to wear them—I had to cut them up for something useful.

Fold two blocks so the X's meet, and stitch them together along one side. Open. The intersecting triangles now form a diamond.

The quilt grew too large to carry. I began piecing strips,
two blocks wide and however many long I needed next, the way
you'd mow a lawn by starting with a central square, zipping off
one side, quarter-turning down the next adjacent row.
But adding on, two blocks too long, so each completed run
begins the next, a spiraling path.

The first time I used solid black. The day he died
stitched in white. Such tiny numbers.

A six-block square section contains 60 inserts. If the finished size
is 48 blocks square, it will hold two thousand
five hundred and twelve inserts.

Because I'm forty now.

Set a one-inch square of any fabric into this diamond. Fold one side of the diamond to lap over the square's edge. Stitch in place.

Elegy. Anniversary. Silk ties, Christmas ribbon, underwear,
a napkin. Mother made a quilt, saved scraps for mine.
Bow Tie. Cathedral Window. Like separate animals
with shared chromosomes. Like windows in adjacent houses.

Repeat with the other three sides.

Because I want to finish it. Yet how satisfying to complete
each strip, drape it over the back of a chair, see how much
I've done. I spend an hour a day on this, sometimes more.
 My new lover drives the car, everywhere we go, so I can quilt.

Because nothing else I've done has felt so wholly mine.

This is the finished window.

The Company We Keep

Half-floating, half-sinking, the crayfish wobbles in the white
plastic dish I yanked from the cupboard and splashed

full of tap water, wobbles intentionless, lifeless. Mindlessly
I jiggle the dish, pluck a glob of wet dog hair from its little

pointy legs. Nothing helps. For this we waded into the cold
Susquehanna, netted ridiculously tiny minnows—all bug eyes

and needle tails—and turned over rocks to catch a crayfish,
two, then three, for the new aquarium. Local shale

stacked into little cave hideouts. The minnows, or whatever
they were, darted in unison like some nervous organism.

The crayfish would snatch up their shrimp pellets with tiny
pincered feet. Then the largest went missing. What fools

we are to kidnap such benign and helpless creatures, cage them
in our homes. It died. It flipped out the back of the aquarium,

thumped to the carpeted floor. Its beady pushpin eyes surveyed
the new terrain: hill of crumpled underwear, marooned ship

of an overturned shoe. Ledges of piled books. The crayfish
hauled its armored body like a slowly fizzing spacesuit

through the deep dark beneath our bed, through our secret
dust and dog hair, tapped its primitive warty claw

along the baseboard while we snored above like careless gods,
oblivious, unrepentant. Now I poke its unresponsive shell—

lolling in the shallow water, I almost believe it's coming back
to life—and now, at last, too late, I think of all the trapped,

forgotten fireflies, the starved, neglected toads; now I cringe
for every "rescued" baby bird I gagged on forcefed worms,

for the worms themselves, for the fermenting jars of tadpoles
floating belly-up on sunny windowsills, the ants, the bugs,

the butterflies: countless, the small ones we've extinguished,
as if we could have been companions, as if we were other

than human, could ever set aside our sorry need for dominion.

Suddenly

A small domestic cloud, pale gray, drifts
above my garden. Now a second cloud.
Like puffs of smoke, this finer dust wind wafts
as heavier winnowed bits rain to the ground.

Not released in trickles through the fingers,
not sown gently like fine seed, but flung
in gritty handfuls, it separates and scatters,
falls back in layers: first the shards of bone,

next grit, then ash, then dust, as if by design,
as if gravity itself could sort
this jumbled riddle. The fuzzed fig leaves, the pine's
sharp needles are coated with this film. It's what

I had to wait three years to do: today
he's been released, and I've a startling joy.

David Speaks in a Dream

Not in sleep are you closest
to the dead. Not in dreams.

It is after making love: the hammering
heart, the incandescent soul, the two

synchronized: the body has focused
almost enough energy

to throw itself away.
I am nearly with you then.

Under

The doctor placed his fists together on my chest,
thumbs up, told me to grab them and hold on
while he counted backward, *like you're a race car
driver,* he said, *ten, nine,* his thumbs warm,
solid in my hands, *eight,* the table undulating,
the round lights wobbling beyond his mask,
seven, the walls swooping in as I clung tight,
slipping out, holding on. It was twenty years
before I recognized this gesture: flung back,
reaching, the man I'd followed home bending
over me with such precision, such absolute
assurance that I gave it up to him, let him take
me where he would, not caring what he did,
knowing he was digging for a part of me that
he could alter, that would retain his imprint all
my life. It had mattered before. Suddenly it
didn't, and I knew that this was how I wished
to die, holding tight, going under; no one
I have ever held has made me feel as safe.

ABOUT THE AUTHOR

Ron Mohring holds a B.A. from the University of Houston and an M.F.A. from Vermont College.

Photo by Cynthia Grace-Lang

His poems have appeared in many journals, including *Alaska Quarterly Review, Artful Dodge, Blue Moon Review, Diagram, The Gettysburg Review, Green Mountains Review, Hanging Loose, Verse Daily* (online) and the premiere issue of *Pool*; in the anthologies *Things Shaped in Passing* (Richard McCann & Michael Klein, eds.) and *Sweet Jesus: Poems About the Ultimate Icon* (Denise Duhamel & Nick Carbó, eds.); and in three chapbooks: *Amateur Grief,* winner of the 1998 Frank O'Hara Award, *The David Museum,* winner of the 2002 New Michigan Press/Diagram Award, and *Beneficence*, co-winner of the 2002 Pecan Grove Press open competition.

He was awarded the 2000 Philip Roth Residency and the 2001-2003 Stadler Fellowship, both at Bucknell University, where he teaches literature and creative writing and serves as Senior Associate Editor of the literary magazine *West Branch*.

ABOUT THE ARTIST

British-born photographer Fred Wilkinson graduated in Fine Arts at London's Goldsmiths College, and was a practicing painter before pursuing a career in art education. He specialized in child art and creativity, and taught art education to postgraduate student teachers at London University for eight years before moving to Cornwall to pursue other interests, including photography.

Fred currently travels extensively in the Far East, studying and collecting traditional and modern ethnic arts and crafts to sell in his world art gallery (www.WorldArtandCrafts.com).

Survivable World is the winner of the 2003 Word Works Washington Prize. Ron Mohring's manuscript was selected from 370 manuscripts submitted by American poets.

FIRST READERS:
Nancy Allinson
Doris Brody
Christopher Conlon
Charlene Conlon
Donald Cunningham
Deanna D'Errico
Michael Gushue
Erich Hintze
James Hopkins
Tod Ibrahim
Lisa Kosow
Sydney March
Mike McDermott
Maggie Rosen
Amy Jo Ross
Jill Tunick
Doug Wilkinson

SECOND READERS:
Brandon Johnson
Miles David Moore
Hilary Tham

FINAL JUDGES:
Karren L. Alenier
J.H. Beall
Bernadette Geyer
Cynthia Hoffman
Ann Rayburn, *Director*

About the Word Works

The Word Works, a nonprofit literary organization, publishes contemporary poetry in collectors' editions. Since 1981, the organization has sponsored the Washington Prize, a $1,500 award to an American poet. Monthly, The Word Works presents free literary programs in the Chevy Chase Café Muse series, and each summer, free poetry programs are held at the historic Joaquin Miller Cabin in Washington, DC's Rock Creek Park. Annually, two high school students debut in the Miller Cabin Series as winners of the Young Poets Competition.

Since 1974, Word Works programs have included: "In the Shadow of the Capitol," a symposium and archival project on the African-American intellectual community in segregated Washington, DC; the Gunston Arts Center Poetry Series (Ai, Carolyn Forché, Stanley Kunitz, and others); the Poet-Editor panel discussions at the Bethesda Writer's Center (John Hollander, Maurice English, Anthony Hecht, Josephine Jacobsen, and others); Poet's Jam, a multi-arts program series featuring poetry in performance; a poetry workshop at the Center for Creative Non-Violence (CCNV) shelter; and the Arts Retreat in Tuscany. Master Class workshops, an ongoing program, have featured Agha Shahid Ali, Thomas Lux, and Marilyn Nelson.

In 2004, Word Works will have published 53 titles, including work from such authors as Deirdra Baldwin, J.H. Beall, Christopher Bursk, John Pauker, Edward Weismiller, and Mac Wellman. Currently, The Word Works publishes books and occasional anthologies under three imprints: the Washington Prize, the Capital Collection, and International Editions.

Past grants have been awarded by the National Endowment for the Arts, National Endowment for the Humanities, DC Commission on the Arts & Humanities, Witter Bynner Foundation, Writer's Center, Bell Atlantic, Batir Foundation, and others, including many generous private patrons.

The Word Works has established an archive of artistic and administrative materials in the Washington Writing Archive housed in the George Washington University Gelman Library.

Please enclose a self-addressed, stamped envelope with all inquiries.

WORD WORKS BOOKS

Karren L. Alenier, *Wandering on the Outside*
Karren L. Alenier, ed., *Whose Woods These Are*
Karren L. Alenier, Hilary Tham, Miles David Moore, eds.,
    Winners: A Retrospective of the Washington Prize
* Nathalie F. Anderson, *Following Fred Astaire*
* Michael Atkinson, *One Hundred Children Waiting for a Train*
Mel Belin, *Flesh That Was Chrysalis* (CAPITAL COLLECTION)
* Peter Blair, *Last Heat*
Doris Brody, *Judging the Distance* (CAPITAL COLLECTION)
Christopher Bursk, ed., *Cool Fire*
Grace Cavalieri, *Pinecrest Rest Haven* (CAPITAL COLLECTION)
Christopher Conlon, *Gilbert and Garbo in Love* (CAPITAL COLLECTION)
Moshe Dor, Barbara Goldberg, Giora Leshem, eds.,
    The Stones Remember
Isaac Goldberg, *Solomon Ibn Gabirol: A Bibliography of His*
    Poems in Translation (INTERNATIONAL EDITIONS)
* Linda Lee Harper, *Toward Desire*
James Hopkins, *Eight Pale Women* (CAPITAL COLLECTION)
* Ann Rae Jonas, *A Diamond Is Hard But Not Tough*
Myong-Hee Kim, *Crow's Eye View: The Infamy of Lee Sang,*
    Korean Poet (INTERNATIONAL EDITIONS)
Vladimir Levchev, *Black Book of the Endangered Species*
    (INTERNATIONAL EDITIONS)
* Fred Marchant, *Tipping Point*
Miles David Moore, *The Bears of Paris* (CAPITAL COLLECTION)
Jacklyn Potter, Dwaine Rieves, Gary Stein, eds.
    Cabin Fever: Poets at Joaquin Miller's Cabin
* Jay Rogoff, *The Cutoff*
Robert Sargent, *Aspects of a Southern Story*
Robert Sargent, *A Woman From Memphis*
* Enid Shomer, *Stalking the Florida Panther*
Maria Terrone, *The Bodies We Were Loaned* (CAPITAL COLLECTION)
Hilary Tham, *Bad Names for Women* (CAPITAL COLLECTION)
Hilary Tham, *Counting* (CAPITAL COLLECTION)
* Miles Waggener, *Phoenix Suites*
* Charlotte Gould Warren, *Gandhi's Lap*
* George Young, *Spinoza's Mouse*

    * Washington Prize winners